Uniquely
Kansas

Larry Bograd

Heinemann Library
Chicago, Illinois

Designed by Heinemann Library
Printed and bound in China by
WKT Company Limited.

08 07 06 05 04
10 9 8 7 6 5 4 3 2 1

**Library of Congress
Cataloging-in-Publication Data**

Bograd, Larry.
   Uniquely Kansas / Larry Bograd.
      v. cm. -- (Heinemann state studies)
Includes bibliographical references and index.
Contents: Uniquely Kansas -- Kansas's geography
and climate -- Famous firsts -- Kansas's state
symbols -- Kansas's history and people -- The
Great Plains -- Kansas's state government --
Kansas's culture -- Kansas's food -- Kansas's folklore
and legends -- Kansas's sports teams -- Kansas's
businesses and products -- Attractions and
landmarks.
   ISBN 1-4034-4654-7 (hc library binding) --
ISBN 1-4034-4723-3
   1. Kansas -- Juvenile literature. [1. Kansas.]
I. Title. II. Series.
   F681.3.B64 2004
   978.1--dc22
                                      2003027151

Cover Pictures

Top (left to right) Dodge City, Amelia
Earhart, Kansas state flag, cattle
Main Sunflowers

Acknowledgments
Development and photo research by
BOOK BUILDERS LLC

The author and publishers are grateful to the
following for permission to reproduce copyrighted
material:

Cover photographs by (top, L–R): Popperfoto/
Alamy; Joe Sohm/Alamy; Sunset Avenue
Productions/Alamy; (main): Kansas Heritage
Center.

Title page (L-R): Courtesy White Castle
Management Co.; Courtesy National Park Service;
Michael C. Snell. Contents: Comstock/Alamy; p. 5,
7, 26T, 30, 34, 44 Michael C. Snell; p. 6 Courtesy
Chris Eberly, DOD Partners in Flight; p. 8, 41, 45
IMA for BOOK BUILDERS LLC; p. 9 Courtesy White
Castle Management Co.; p. 10, 18, 19, 21T, 21B,
23T, 40B, 42T Kansas State Historical Society;
p. 11 Courtesy U.S. Senate Historical Office;
p. 12T Joe Sohm/Alamy; p. 12B One Mile Up;
p. 14T Alamy; p. 14B USDA Forest Service; p. 15T
Agricultural Research Center; p. 15M Graphic
Science/Alamy; p. 15B Gay Bumgarner/Alamy;
p. 16T USFWS/Washington, D.C. Library; p. 16B
USFWS; p. 23B Hulton; p. 24 Rob Crandall/Alamy;
p. 25 Grant Heilman Photography; p. 26B NPS;
p. 28 Courtesy Greater Topeka Chamber of
Commerce; p. 29 Courtesy Topeka Convention &
Visitors Bureau; p. 30 Courtesy Red Brick Road
Promotions; p. 31 Sunset Avenue Productions/
Alamy; p. 32 Jim Turner; p. 33 B. Minton/
Heinemann Library; p. 35 R. Capozzelli/
Heinemann Library; p. 36 Courtesy KUAC; p. 37T
AP Photo; p. 37B Courtesy Harlem Globetrotters;
p. 38 Courtesy Raytheon Aircraft Co.; p. 39
Comstock/Alamy; p. 40T Popperfoto/Alamy; p. 43
Courtesy Jeanet Bean/Fick Fossil & History
Museum

Special thanks to Allan Tanner of the Kansas State
Historical Society for his expert review during the
preparation of this book.

Every effort has been made to contact copyright
holders of any material reproduced in this book.
Any omissions will be rectified in subsequent
printings if notice is given to the publisher.

Some words are shown in bold, **like this.**
You can find out what they mean by looking
in the glossary.

Contents

Uniquely Kansas

Unique means one of a kind. One way that Kansas is unique is that it has a place inside its borders, Meade's Ranch in Smith County, that is the geographical center of the 48 **contiguous** states that make up the United States mainland. Kansas is known as "The Wheat State" because it is the leading producer of wheat in the country.

Many people think Kansas is flat. However, it is actually tilted. The western part of the state is about 4,000 feet above sea level. The eastern part is about 700 feet above sea level. That means a person driving through Kansas from west to east will actually go downhill almost two-thirds of a mile.

ORIGIN OF THE STATE'S NAME

Kansas is named after the Native American tribe Kansa. The Kansa people lived in the region when fur trappers from the eastern part of the United States first arrived in the early 1830s. *Kansa* comes from the Lakota word meaning "south wind people." The Kansa were probably named this because they lived in a windy part of present-day Kansas.

MAJOR CITIES

All of Kansas's large cities are located in the eastern half of the state. The largest cities are Topeka, Wichita, and Kansas City.

Topeka, the capital of Kansas, has a population of 122,000. It is located west of Kansas City along Interstate 70. Topeka comes from a Native American word meaning "a good place to grow potatoes." Potatoes are no longer important to Topeka, but shoes are. Payless Shoe Stores are based in Topeka. This national chain of shoe stores, the largest in the Western Hemisphere, sells more than 200 million pairs of shoes each year.

The largest city in Kansas is Wichita, with a population of 344,000. It was named after the Wichita people who once lived there. The sunny weather and flat land make Wichita a good place to fly airplanes.

In 1903 the Wright brothers became the first people to successfully fly an airplane. By 1908, people were flying **dirigibles** and airplanes in Wichita. Today, Wichita is called the "Air Capital of the World," because more airplanes and jets are built there, by such companies as Beechcraft, Cessna, Learjet, and Boeing, than anywhere else in the world.

The state's second-largest city is Kansas City. There is another Kansas City located across the Missouri River, in Missouri. Kansas City, Kansas, has a population of 147,000. The greater Kansas City area, including the Missouri side, has more than 1.9 million people. Kansas City is unique because it represents two different cities in two states that share the same name.

In Kansas City, large numbers of people are employed by Sprint, General Motors, the University of Kansas Medical Center and the government.

Kansas's Geography and Climate

Kansas forms a nearly perfect rectangle. It contains hills, valleys, flat plains, and rolling prairies of long and short grasses. The state also has canyons, sand dunes, and swamps. Kansas is divided into three major land regions: the Dissected Till Plains, the Southeastern Plains, and the Great Plains.

LAND

The Dissected Till Plains covers several midwestern states, including northeastern Kansas. The region was formed when an **Ice Age** glacier melted and left rich soil called till. Millions of years ago, rivers and streams cut through, or dissected, the region, creating high **bluffs** and rolling hills of forests.

The Southeastern Plains extend west from the Missouri River to the center of Kansas. This area includes gently rolling hills. Tall bluestem grasses grow wild, which provide cattle with many of the nutrients they need. Thus,

This highlighted section of the Midwest is called the Dissected Till Plains, which has some of the richest farmland in the counrty.

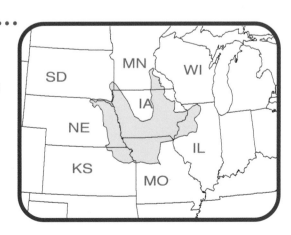

6

it is one of the best places in the world to raise cattle. Wichita is located in the Southeastern Plains.

The Great Plains makes up the western half of Kansas. The Great Plains resulted, in part, from **erosion,** or soil from the Rocky Mountains blown east by the wind. At the western Kansas border is Mount Sunflower, which at 4,039 feet above sea level is the highest point in the state. The **elevation** drops to about 1,500 feet above sea level on the eastern side of the Great Plains.

The Great Plains is a gently rolling landscape, similar to the Southeastern Plains but at a higher elevation. Several rivers flow from west to east across the Great Plains, including the Arkansas, Smoky Hill, and Saline rivers. (People in Kansas call the Arkansas River the Ar-*Kansas* River instead of the *Arkan*-saw River.)

CLIMATE

Climate is the pattern of an area's wind, temperature, and precipitation, or amount of water. Weather is what is happening at a given moment.

Kansas has a temperate continental climate. Temperate means it is rarely, if ever, very hot or very cold. Continental means that Kansas is in the middle of the country, away from an ocean that might affcct its weather.

Kansas's climate differs by region. Eastern Kansas has more rain and is more humid than the rest of the state. The central part has the most wind. The western part is the driest and sunniest. Kansas has four distinct seasons, with an average annual temperature of 55°F. Spring is mostly mild with periods of rain. Summer is hot and dry, with temperatures at times topping 100°F. Fall is cool and pleasant during the day, but it becomes increasingly cold at night. Winter brings snow

Long, hot, dry summers make Kansas an ideal place to grow corn.

and an average temperature of about 28°F, but sometimes it dips below 0°F, which is cold enough to freeze rivers.

Kansas is often very windy because of its location on the Great Plains. Strong winds blow southward from Canada across the central part of the United States. This land is flat; there are no mountains, hills, or other natural barriers to stop the winds.

Kansas is often home to tornadoes, particularly in early summer. On average, 39 tornadoes touch down in Kansas each year. Only Texas and Oklahoma have more tornadoes than Kansas. The deadliest tornado in Kansas' history happened on May 25, 1955. It hit the small town of Udall and killed 80 people.

Annual precipitation varies from more than 40 inches in southeastern Kansas to less than 20 inches in the western part of the state near the Colorado border.

Average Annual Precipitation
Kansas

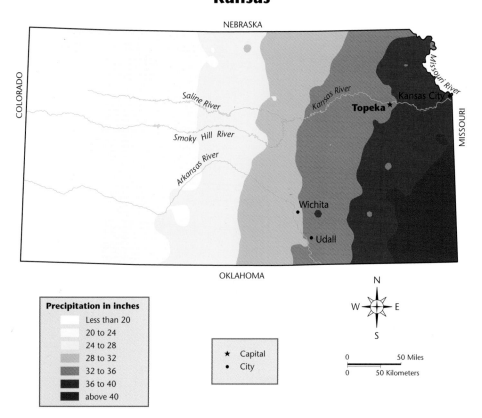

NEBRASKA

COLORADO

Saline River

Kansas River

Kansas City

Topeka ★

MISSOURI

Missouri River

Smoky Hill River

Arkansas River

Wichita

• Udall

OKLAHOMA

Precipitation in inches

	Less than 20
	20 to 24
	24 to 28
	28 to 32
	32 to 36
	36 to 40
	above 40

★ Capital
• City

N
W — E
S

0   50 Miles
0   50 Kilometers

Famous Firsts

FAMOUS FOOD FIRSTS

In 1919 Tom Henry from Arkansas City invented the O'Henry candy bar. Its original name was "Tom Henry," but it was changed when the Curtis Candy Company bought the idea. O'Henry candy bars are now produced by Nestlé.

White Castle, the first fast-food restaurant in the nation, opened in Wichita in 1921. It served hamburgers for five cents. To start this business, founder E.W. "Billy" Ingram borrowed $700. Eventually, White Castle's small cement castles were built in many places across the country. Today, there are about 380 White Castle restaurants in the United States.

The first fast-food restaurants looked like miniature castles. They were painted white to highlight the company's cleanliness.

FAMOUS BUSINESS FIRSTS

In 1835 the first newspaper in North America printed entirely in a Native American language began in Shawnee. It was named the *Siwinowe Kesibwi,* or *Shawnee Sun.*

In 1905 Kansas University scientists were the first to find helium in natural gas. Helium is used to keep balloons

The Birth of Pizza Hut

On June 15, 1958, Wichita brothers Frank and Dan Carney borrowed $600 from their mother and opened the very first Pizza Hut in the country. It was named "Pizza Hut" because the name fit on the sign left by the building's previous owner. By 1968 there were 300 Pizza Huts in the United States and Canada. In 1977 the company was sold to PepsiCo, the parent company of Pepsi Cola. Pizza Hut is now the largest pizza restaurant company in the world, with 12,000 outlets in 90 countries.

afloat and to make computer processors. The discovery led to the commercial helium industry. Today, Kansas leads the nation in the production of helium.

Lutie Lytle was born in Topeka in 1874. She became the first African American woman to practice law in the United States.

Virgil Coffer of Ransom invented the world's first riding lawn mower. He named it the "Virginia Wonder Mower," partly in honor of his first name. To make people aware of his invention, he rode it coast to coast in 1952.

In 1954 David D. Blanton of Wichita invented the autopilot, which allows a pilot to set controls so a plane will fly by itself on a steady course and at a constant speed. The autopilot allows pilots to briefly rest or to tend to other tasks.

FAMOUS FIRSTS FOR KANSAS WOMEN

Lucy Hobbs Taylor became the first woman to graduate from a dental college, the Ohio College of Dental Surgery. She moved to

Kansas in 1867 and became the state's first female dentist.

The first woman mayor in the United States was Susanna Madora Salter, who was elected in Argonia in 1887. She was 27 years old.

From 1991 to 1995, when Joan Finney served as governor, Kansas was the first state to have a woman governor, a woman senator (Nancy Landon Kassebaum), and a woman U.S. representative (Jan Meyers) at the same time.

Nancy Landon Kassebaum was the first woman to be elected to the U.S. Senate.

The Mystery of Amelia Earhart

Amelia Earhart mysteriously disappeared in 1937 while trying to fly around the world. Amelia Earhart was born on July 24, 1897, in Atchison. At age 23, Earhart had her first ride in an airplane. "By the time I had got two or three hundred feet off the ground," she said, "I knew I had to fly." On May 20, 1932, she became the first woman to fly solo across the Atlantic Ocean. Three years later, she became the first person to fly solo across the Pacific Ocean, from Honolulu, Hawaii, to Oakland, California. As she approached her 40th birthday in 1937, she wanted to become the first woman to fly around the world. She left Miami on June 1, heading west with her navigator Fred Noonan. Four weeks later, they were three-fourths done with their 29,000-mile trip. They were flying from island to island in the Pacific Ocean, but one day in July they did not reach the tiny strip of land named Howland Island. On July 19, after using ships and planes to search 250,000 square miles of ocean, the U.S. government decided that Earhart was gone forever.

Kansas's State Symbols

KANSAS STATE FLAG

The Kansas flag, adopted in 1927, consists of the state seal centered on a dark blue background. The state flower, the sunflower, rests on a bar of twisted gold above the seal. Across the top of the seal are 34 stars, indicating that Kansas was the 34th state to join the Union.

The state flag is flown above all official state buildings.

The Kansas state seal is used on all official documents issued by the state government.

KANSAS STATE SEAL

The Great Seal of the State of Kansas dates from 1861. The right-hand corner of the seal shows the sun rising in the east, which represents the promise of a new day. To the left is a steamboat moving down a river, which represents commerce. In the center are a settler's cabin and a farmer plowing a field with a pair of horses, which represent agriculture. Behind the cabin is a wagon train heading west. Off in the distance, two Native Americans on horseback hunt a herd of bison. Around the top of the seal is the state motto beneath a cluster of 34 stars.

STATE MOTTO: *"AD ASTRA PER ASPERA"*

The motto *Ad Astra per Aspera* appears on the state seal and flag. It is Latin for "To the stars through difficulties." It refers to the years before 1861, when Kansas became a state. At that time it was unclear whether Kansas would be a slave state or a free state.

STATE NICKNAME: THE JAYHAWK STATE

Kansas enjoys several nicknames, including "The Sunflower State," "The Wheat State," and the "The Jayhawk State." A jayhawk is a mythical bird, part jay and part hawk—two birds known as fearless fighters. The term originated during the 1850s, when people from Kansas who were opposed to **slavery** went to Missouri to free slaves and bring them back to Kansas. These raiders became known as jayhawks.

STATE SONG: "HOME ON THE RANGE"

Kansas's state song is one of the most well-known songs in the country. "Home on the Range" was taken from a poem by Dr. Brewster M. Higley, a pioneer living in Smith County, Kansas, in 1871. It became the Kansas state song in 1947.

STATE FLOWER: SUNFLOWER

Because it is found throughout Kansas, the sunflower became the state flower in 1903

"Home on the Range"

Oh, give me a home, where the buffalo roam,
Where the deer and the antelope play,
Where seldom is heard a discouraging word,
And the skies are not cloudy all day.
Home, home on the range,
Where the deer and the antelope play,
Where seldom is heard a discouraging word,
And the skies are not cloudy all day.
Where the air is so pure, the zephyrs so free,
The breezes so balmy and light,
That I would not exchange my home on the range
For all the cities so bright.

after being selected by the state **legislature.** Ancient people turned this wildflower into a crop, harvesting its seeds to roast and eat. Today, oil produced from the sunflower is used in cooking.

STATE BIRD: WESTERN MEADOWLARK

The western meadowlark was adopted as the Kansas state bird in 1925. It is one of the most common birds found in Kansas. Meadowlarks make their nests on the ground. They weave dried grasses into a bowl shape. A female lays an average of five eggs twice a year.

STATE TREE: COTTONWOOD

The eastern cottonwood became Kansas's state tree in 1937. It has a shallow but extensive root system, which is well adapted to the prairie. Cottonwoods can live more than 100 years. Cottonwoods provided shade and wood for early settlers. Because cottonwoods grow along creeks, rivers, and streams, their presence means that water is likely nearby.

Cottonwoods are related to poplars and aspens. These trees grow quickly and have leaves that shake and shimmer in the wind. Their seed pods contain a cushion that looks like cotton, which is why people named this tree the cottonwood.

STATE ANIMAL: BISON

Bison are often called the American Buffalo. Bison bulls, or males, may weigh up to 2,000 pounds. Cows, or females, may weigh around 1,100 pounds, and calves weigh about 65 pounds at birth. Bison live about twenty years. In the mid-1800s there were hundreds of thousands of bison in Kansas, but most were killed by hunters hired by railroad companies. The bison became the state animal in 1955.

The number of bison in Kansas has increased because ranches are replacing cattle with bison. Bison are raised for their meat, which has less fat than beef does.

STATE INSECT: HONEYBEE

Honeybees produce honey from nectar gathered from flowers. Honey is an important part of Kansas's agriculture, so the state legislature selected the honeybee in 1976 as the state insect.

STATE REPTILE: ORNATE BOX TURTLE

The ornate box turtle became the Kansas state reptile in 1986. This common reptile of the prairie lives on land and has a colorful pattern on its shell. Males have orange or red eyes and orange or red faces, necks, and front legs. Females are yellow in these areas. These turtles eat insects, worms, spiders, and berries that have fallen to the ground. They can live for more than twenty years.

Honeybees are extremely important to the process of pollination, which allows fruits, vegetables, and other plant-life to grow and reproduce.

The age of an ornate box turtle can be determined by counting the number of growth rings on the bottom of its shell.

Barred tiger salamanders may live to be twenty years old. They can grow up to fourteen inches long, which is big enough to eat a mouse.

STATE AMPHIBIAN: BARRED TIGER SALAMANDER

Barred tiger salamanders are difficult to find in the wild. They mostly come out on cool nights. They have many yellow spots between their front and hind legs. Although they live on land, they lay their eggs in water, like other amphibians. In 1994 after schoolchildren worked to make the salamander the Kansas state amphibian, the legislature made it official.

STATE ROCK: LIMESTONE

Limestone is found where ancient seas once covered the land. As the seas dried up, the remains of plants and animals became pressed together. Over millions of years, these remains became large slabs of limestone, which is plentiful in northwestern Kansas and popular building material. More than 100 years ago, people in Kansas cut fence posts from limestone.

STATE FISH: CHANNEL CATFISH

The channel catfish was selected as the state fish in 2003. It gets its name from the eight barbels, or whiskers, on either side of its mouth. The largest catfish caught in Kansas weighed nearly 35 pounds. A group of students hoped that having an official fish would make people more aware of the state's large catfish industry.

Catfish eat smaller animals and plants found on the bottom of streams, rivers, and lakes. They find food by searching the bottom with their whiskers.

Kansas's History and People

The vast plains and rich grasslands of what we now call Kansas brought the first people to the area. These people hunted and raised crops.

EARLY HISTORY

Humans have lived in present-day Kansas for about 15,000 years. In the early 1500s Spanish explorers came from Mexico to Kansas in search of gold. There they found Native American tribes, including the Wichita, Pawnee, Kiowa, and Kansa people. These Native Americans followed bison herds, using the animal for food and fur. The Spanish explorers failed to find gold and did not stay in the area, leaving the area to Native Americans for almost 300 years.

LEWIS AND CLARK

In 1803 President Thomas Jefferson convinced the U.S. Congress to purchase from France an enormous amount of land that stretched west from the Mississippi River to the Rocky Mountains. This land became known as the **Louisiana Territory,** and it doubled the size of the United States. Part of this territory became present-day Kansas.

That same year, Jefferson sent a team led by William Clark and Meriwether Lewis to explore and **survey** the new territory, all the way to the Pacific Ocean. The men charted the natural resources and determined if the land was suitable for farming. Between June 26 and July 10, 1804, the Lewis and Clark expedition visited present-day Kansas, camping where the Kansas and Missouri rivers meet. They reported that the land was not good for growing crops and discouraged settlement. Today, people in

Kansas find this amusing, because the state is often called "The Wheat State" and "The Breadbasket of the World."

BLEEDING KANSAS AND STATEHOOD

In the 1820s thousands of people from the eastern states began to move west, wanting to start farms and new towns. Many traveled through Kansas, and some found land suitable for farming and decided to stay. This, in turn, led to disputes between the settlers and Native Americans, because the settlers built homes and fences on what had been Native American land. The U.S. government decided in the late 1820s to build forts to keep the peace and to protect travelers. Towns in eastern Kansas surrounding Fort Leavenworth soon followed.

In 1854 Congress established the Kansas Territory. At the time, it stretched west into present-day Colorado. During the first half of the 1800s, the question of **slavery** dominated national political life. Like the rest of the nation, people in the Kansas Territory were divided into groups of those who were in favor of slavery and those who were against slavery. Congress gave the people of the territory the right to decide whether to join the Union as a free state that outlawed slavery or as a slave state that allowed it.

People's feelings were so strong on both sides of the slavery issue that Kansas became known as "Bleeding Kansas" because of the violent battles involving settlers who tried to permit slavery and those who were determined to prevent it.

At the time, the nation had an equal number of proslavery and antislavery states. In this way, the free states and the slave states had the same number of Senators in the U.S. Congress. Neither side could overrule the other. Kansas became important because it would tip the balance in favor of either the free states or the slave states. Between 1854 and 1861 more than 200 people died in Kansas as proslavery and antislavery groups fought for control of the territorial government. This government would determine whether Kansas would enter the Union as a free state or a slave state. Finally, on January 29, 1861, the bill making Kansas the 34th state reached President James Buchanan's desk and he signed it, officially making Kansas a free state.

John Brown

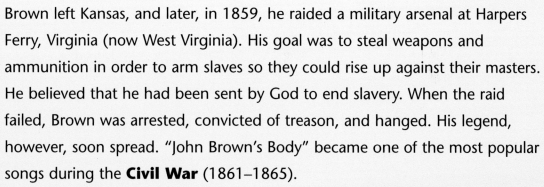

As a boy growing up in Ohio, John Brown (1800–1859) saw a slave being beaten with a shovel. The sight never left Brown, who later became a dedicated—and violent—opponent of slavery. In 1856 during the peak of violence over the issue of slavery in Kansas, Brown and his followers killed five proslavery supporters near Pottawatomie Creek, about 30 miles south of present-day Kansas City. Afterward, Brown left Kansas, and later, in 1859, he raided a military arsenal at Harpers Ferry, Virginia (now West Virginia). His goal was to steal weapons and ammunition in order to arm slaves so they could rise up against their masters. He believed that he had been sent by God to end slavery. When the raid failed, Brown was arrested, convicted of treason, and hanged. His legend, however, soon spread. "John Brown's Body" became one of the most popular songs during the **Civil War** (1861–1865).

THE CIVIL WAR (1861–1865)

When the Civil War began in 1861, Kansas was the newest state in the Union. This did not stop it from sending more than 20,000 men to serve in the Union army. This figure represents two-thirds of the adult male population at that time. Only one major Civil War battle took place in Kansas. In October 1864 the Union won the Battle of Mine Creek, south of present-day Kansas City. The victory was important because it kept Kansas under Union control—and kept it a free state.

TOWARD A MODERN STATE

After the Civil War ended, Kansas witnessed its greatest period of population growth. Among the people drawn to Kansas in the second half of the 1800s were freed slaves. Between 1870 and 1880 more than 20,000 African Americans moved to the state from southern states. They were called Exodusters, a name that came from the word *exodus*. Exodus means a large movement of people from one place to another.

Between 1860 and 1890 Kansas's population rose from about 100,000 people to nearly 1.5 million. This growth was due in part to the rapid expansion of the Union Pacific Railroad. People and goods could travel easily across the state, leading to the growth of such towns as Wichita, Dodge City, and Abilene.

URBANIZATION

While many people think of Kansas as a rural state, 90 percent of its people live in cities. This move to urban life gained strength in the early 1900s. The discovery of oil and natural gas helped to fuel the state economy, as they powered new factories built in Wichita and other cities.

The 1930s saw years of horrible **drought.** Kansas became part of the **Dust Bowl,** which stretched from

Brown v. Board of Education of Topeka, Kansas

In 1951 Linda Brown, a young African-American girl, tried to attend her local school in Topeka. Although the neighborhood was racially mixed, the school was all white. Linda and the other African-American children were expected to travel across town to attend an all-black school. Her father and twelve other parents hired a lawyer and sued the Topeka Board of Education, asking it to end racial **segregation.** The case went all the way up to the U.S. Supreme Court, which heard the case in 1954. The Supreme Court, ruling in favor of Linda Brown, declared that segregation, or the separation of the races, in public schools was unlawful.

North Dakota to Texas. The lack of rain caused many farms to fail. Needing to make a living, farmers seeking factory jobs moved to cities. However, the 1930s saw extremely bad economic times around the world, including the United States. This period became known as the Great Depression, during which many factories and business failed. It was not until **World War II** (1941–1945) that Kansas and the rest of the country began to recover.

FAMOUS PEOPLE

Carry Nation (1846–1911), leader of anti-alcohol movement. Born in Kentucky in 1846, Carry Nation moved to Kansas in 1890. Ten years later, dressed in a long black dress, she led a national crusade against "demon liquor."

Carry Nation's home in Medicine Lodge, in southwestern Kansas, is now a National Historic Landmark. It contains many of her personal belongings, including one of her famous hatchets.

She became known for entering saloons and destroying bottles of liquor with a hatchet.

George Washington Carver (1860–1943), inventor. Born a slave in Missouri, George Washington Carver moved to Kansas at about age ten and later attended high school there. After attending college in Iowa, he was convinced by the African-American leader Booker T. Washington to come to the Tuskegee Institute in Alabama to teach and to do research. Carver spent his remaining years there. He invented hundreds of uses for the peanut and other southern crops, including using it in paint, cosmetics, and ink.

Clyde Cessna (1879–1954), aviation pioneer. Born in Hawthorne, Iowa, Clyde Cessna built and flew his first plane in 1911. In 1925 he founded the Travel Air Company in Wichita, which built planes. Three years later, he changed the name to Cessna Aircraft. Today, it is one of the world's largest makers of general aviation aircraft. The small propeller planes and jets are used by individuals and businesses.

Walter Johnson (1887–1946), baseball player. Pitcher Walter Johnson was born in Humboldt. Because he stood six feet, one inch tall and weighed 200 pounds, he was nicknamed "The Big Train." He played 21 seasons for the Washington Senators. He is second on the Major League's all-time win list with 416 victories, and he holds the Major League record for career shutouts with 110. In 1913 he pitched 56 consecutive scoreless innings. In 1936 he became one of the first five players selected to the Baseball Hall of Fame.

Langston Hughes (1902–1967), poet. Langston Hughes, an African American, became famous as part of the 1920s **Harlem Renaissance,** centered in New York City. Hughes spent his boyhood in Lawrence and Topeka. Rather than imitate traditional poetry, Hughes used the rhythms of African-American music and speech in such poems as "The Negro Speaks of Rivers," and the poetry collection *Montage of a Dream Deferred.*

Vivian Vance (1909–1979), actress. Born in Cherryvale, Vivian Vance was best known for playing Ethel Mertz on the TV show *I Love Lucy* from 1951 to 1957. Ethel and Lucy were best friends and neighbors on the long-running show. They often got into trouble together, frustrating their husbands Fred and Ricky.

Gordon Parks (1912–   ), photographer. Born in Fort Scott, Gordon Parks overcame poverty, racial **discrimination,** and a lack of formal education to become a photographer, filmmaker, writer, and composer. His novel *The Learning Tree* later became a movie, which he directed. In 1971 he directed the movie *Shaft,* about an African-American detective.

Gwendolyn Brooks (1917–2000), poet. Gwendolyn Brooks was born in Topeka. She is best known for writing about African-American urban life. Her books include *Children Coming Home* (1991), *Riot*

*In 1954 Vivian Vance became the first actress to be awarded an **Emmy Award** for best supporting actress for her role as Ethel Mertz on the show* I Love Lucy.

In 1950 Gwendolyn Brooks became the first African American to win a Pulitzer Prize.

*Senator Bob Dole was elected to Congress after coming home to Kansas a wounded **World War II** veteran. A German soldier firing a machine gun injured Dole's right arm. Dole never recovered use of his arm.*

(1969), *The Bean Eaters* (1960), and *Annie Allen* (1949), for which she received the **Pulitzer Prize.**

Bob Dole (1923–), politician. Born in the small town of Russell in western Kansas, Bob Dole became a leader of the Republican Party in the 1980s and 1990s. He served as a U.S. Representative for seven years, beginning in 1961. In 1968 he was elected to the U.S. Senate, where he served for 28 years. In 1996 he ran unsuccessfully for president against Bill Clinton.

Barry Sanders (1968–), football player. Born in Wichita, Barry Sanders won the Heisman Trophy for the best college player of 1988. During his three years at Oklahoma State, he set thirteen National Collegiate Athletic Association (NCAA) season records. He joined the Detroit Lions in 1989 and became the first National Football League (NFL) player to run for 1,500 yards for three straight seasons and 1,000 yards for the first eight seasons. In 1997 Sanders became the third running back to run for more than 2,000 yards in one season. He is the NFL's third all-time leading rusher.

The Great Plains

The Great Plains stretch east to west from Ohio to Colorado and north to south from Canada to Mexico. The Great Plains occupy the middle third of North America. Scientists refer to the Great Plains as grasslands or prairies. Grasslands are large open spaces with few bushes. Trees are found near rivers and streams only.

THE UNTOUCHED PRAIRIE

The Kansas prairie is called a mixed-grass prairie because the grass grows two to three feet tall. In tallgrass prairies, grass grows up to five feet tall. In short-grass prairies, the grass rarely reaches two feet in height.

North America was once covered with over 400,000 square miles of tallgrass prairie. Today, however, less than 16,000 square miles remain. This prairieland is primarily in Kansas.

The Return of the Bison

Bison were once the most abundant grazing animal in North America, with more than 70 million living across the middle of the continent. Native Americans hunted the bison for food. Between 1860 and 1880, as settlers and the railroad moved west across Kansas and the Great Plains, gunmen slaughtered the great bison herds. By 1889 fewer than 600 bison remained alive. For most of the 1900s, the bison was near **extinction. Conservationist** groups, working with ranchers and government officials, have taken steps to reestablish the bison. Bison have replaced cattle on some ranches, and laws protect the bison from being hunted or killed.

TALLGRASS PRAIRIE NATIONAL PRESERVE

In 1996 the U.S. Congress established the Tallgrass Prairie National Preserve in south-central Kansas, near Strong City. It is the only unit of the National Park Service dedicated to preserving a section of tallgrass prairie. The 10,894-acre preserve is made up of rolling hills of grass interrupted by streams and creeks. The preserve is open to visitors year round.

The Tallgrass Prairie National Preserve is home to 31 different types of mammals, including bison and antelope, 130 kinds of birds, about 400 different plants, and numerous reptiles and insects.

Kansas's State Government

Kansas's state government is modeled after the U.S. government. It has three branches—the legislative branch, the executive branch, and the judicial branch.

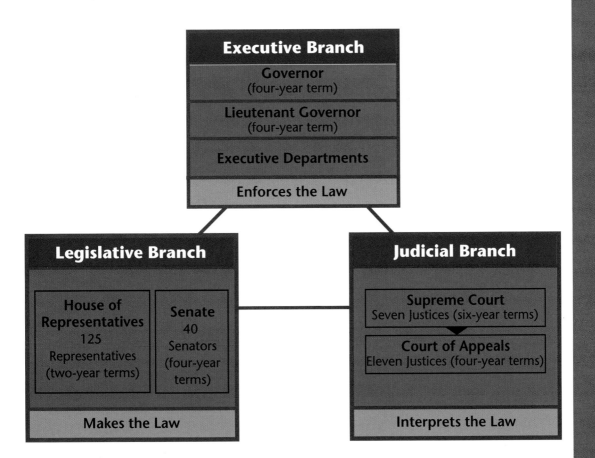

Executive Branch

Governor
(four-year term)

Lieutenant Governor
(four-year term)

Executive Departments

Enforces the Law

Legislative Branch

House of Representatives
125 Representatives
(two-year terms)

Senate
40 Senators
(four-year terms)

Makes the Law

Judicial Branch

Supreme Court
Seven Justices (six-year terms)

Court of Appeals
Eleven Justices (four-year terms)

Interprets the Law

LEGISLATIVE BRANCH

Kansas's **legislature** makes the laws for the state. It is also responsible for raising the money to pay for state services by passing **tax** laws.

The Kansas state capitol was completed in 1904 after 37 years of construction.

The Kansas legislature is divided into two houses. The larger body, which has 125 members, is called the House of Representatives. State representatives are elected by voters and serve two-year terms. The smaller body, known as the Senate, has 40 members who are elected to four-year terms.

The Kansas legislature meets in the capitol in Topeka. After the legislature passes a **bill,** it goes to the governor who must sign it to make it a law.

Executive Branch

The executive branch is led by the governor. The governor is elected in even numbered years without presidential elections by a statewide vote to a term of four years. The governor prepares a state budget, recommending to the legislature how to spend public money. The governor

Kansas's Constitutions

Because of the battle over whether Kansas would be a slave state or a free state, it took several attempts for Kansas's voters to decide on a state constitution. A constitution states how a government is organized and what laws the government must enforce. In December 1857 proslavery forces met in the territorial capital of Lecompton in northeastern Kansas and passed the Lecompton Constitution. President James Buchanan urged the U.S. Congress to admit Kansas under this constitution as a proslavery state, but his efforts failed. It took three more attempts before Kansas's voters approved a no-slavery constitution. This constitution became the basis of law once Kansas entered the Union.

also approves or rejects bills passed by the legislature. Other state officials include the lieutenant governor who is second in command to the governor, the attorney general who enforces state laws, and the secretary of state who keeps state records. Like the governor, these executive officers are elected to four-year terms.

Organized in 1855 with Topeka as the county seat, Shawnee County was carved out of what was Shawnee Indian lands. Topeka is now the capital.

JUDICIAL BRANCH

The judicial branch decides on the meaning of the laws that are passed by the legislature and enforced by the executive branch.

The district courts, organized at the county level, hear civil and criminal cases. Civil cases center on disagreements between people or companies. Criminal cases involve a charge of breaking a law. Most municipal and district judges are elected by local voters.

The **appellate court** hears appeals cases only. In the appellate courts, a panel of three judges hears each case and reaches a decision. There is not a **jury.** The court of appeals reviews decisions made by district courts, which means that they may overturn, or change, the district courts' decisions if there is a good reason to do so. The governor appoints court of appeals justices, and voters decide every four years whether to keep them in office.

The Kansas Supreme Court is the highest court in the state. It has the final say in legal matters. The chief justice heads the court and is responsible for the court system. Like the appellate court, the Kansas Supreme Court mostly hears appeals. The governor appoints state supreme court justices for a term of six years, and the voters must approve them every six years to remain in office.

Kansas's Culture

Kansas's culture reflects its strong agricultural traditions. The parents or grandparents of many Kansans lived on farms or in small farming towns.

Kansas farmers plant wheat each fall and harvest it early in the summer.

CATTLE RANCHING

In 1867 Abilene, in north-central Kansas, became famous as the place where the Chisholm Cattle Trail ended. Railroad trains waited there to take longhorn cattle, brought up or driven from Texas ranches to slaugh-

Kansas and the Wizard of Oz

One of the most famous books and movies that takes place in Kansas was written by a man who never lived there. L. Frank Baum was born in Chittenango, New York, in 1856. He became a newspaperman in 1880 and worked in South Dakota and Chicago. However, he is best known for writing *The Wonderful Wizard of Oz,* published in 1900. The book launched a series of books about the mythical Oz, which first became a stage musical and later a 1939 movie, *The Wizard of Oz.* Many people's impressions of Kansas are based on the scenes of Dorothy and her aunt and uncle on their Kansas farm, where a twister, or tornado, carries Dorothy and her dog, Toto, to Oz. In reality the scenes were shot on a Hollywood movie set.

terhouses across the Midwest. Like other cattle towns of the 1860s and 1870s, Abilene was a lawless settlement on the Western frontier. Famous lawmen such as James "Wild Bill" Hickok (1837–1876) were brought in to maintain the peace.

GERMAN–RUSSIAN WHEAT FARMERS

In the 1770s thousands of people left war-torn Germany, settled in Russia, and began farming wheat. A hundred years later, in the 1870s, many of these same families left Russia and moved to the United States, seeking religious freedom. By 1879 about 12,000 German–Russians lived in Kansas. Today, their German–Russian culture may be found in several counties in central Kansas, including Marion, Harvey, McPherson, Ellis, Russell, and Rush counties.

Western Kansas is dry and does not lend itself to growing crops. Instead, people raise cattle and other livestock.

Kansas's Food

Kansas's favorite foods are two of its most important products, beef and wheat. Kansas has almost three cows for every person. The state also produces about one-fifth of the nation's wheat. The wheat is often milled into flour and used in baked goods. Another important crop is sunflower seed.

EUROPEAN TRADITIONS

Europeans who settled in Kansas brought their foods with them. Today, German, Swedish, Czech, and Swiss dishes remain popular. Foods such as sausage, sauerkraut, beets, and dumplings are favorites. Sauerkraut is

Lindsborg is often called Little Sweden because of the many Swedish immigrants who settled there beginning in 1868. Favorite foods in Lindsborg include potato sausage, meatballs, and a dessert bread called Swedish tea rings.

a flavorful dish made from shredded cabbage that has been salted and fermented. Pork sausage and sauerkraut is a traditional meal served on New Year's in many German immigrant households. It is said to bring good luck for the coming year.

Sunflower Chippers

Always be sure to bake with an adult's help.

Ingredients

2 cups all-purpose flour

1/2 teaspoon cream of tartar

1/2 teaspoon baking soda

1/2 cup shortening

1/2 cup sugar

1/2 cup brown sugar

1/2 cup chocolate chips

2 tablespoons whole sunflower seeds

1/3 cup sunflower oil

1 egg

1/2 cup dry roasted sunflower seeds
   (shelled)

(shelled)

In a medium bowl, sift flour with cream of tartar and baking soda; set aside. In a large bowl, beat shortening, sugars, and oil until light and fluffy. Add egg; beat for 3 minutes. Stir in flour mixture and sunflower seeds until well combined. Shape into 1-inch balls. Place balls 2 inches apart on an ungreased cookie sheet. Decorate with a chocolate chip in the center and five whole sunflower seeds fashioned in a spoke pattern. Bake in a 350°F oven 12 to 13 minutes or until golden brown. Remove to wire rack and cool. Makes 60 cookies.

Kansas's Folklore and Legends

Legends and folklore are stories that are not totally true but are often based on bits of truth. These stories helped people understand things that could not be easily explained. They also taught lessons to younger generations. All peoples have passed down stories as part of their culture.

Greenbush Day is held here at the St. Aloysius Historical Site every year.

THE LEGEND OF GREENBUSH

In 1869 in the little southeastern Kansas town of Greenbush, a priest named Father Phillip Colleton was caught in a horrible storm. The sky filled with lightning and thunder. Father Colleton was pelted with hail, and he realized there was no way he could ride to safety. So he got off his horse, removed the saddle, and freed the frightened animal. The priest covered himself as best he could with the saddle. He prayed that if his life were spared, he would build a church on that

Pecos Bill was the greatest cowboy of them all—at least according to Pecos Bill!

spot. The storm soon passed, and Father Colleton kept his word. He built a wooden church in the same spot in 1871. Six years later, it was destroyed in a storm. The church was rebuilt in 1881 and was later replaced with a new, larger one. However, in 1982 it was struck by lightning and burned again. The church has since been renovated into a place of worship.

PECOS BILL RIDES A TORNADO

The legendary cowboy Pecos Bill claimed he could ride anything. No horse or bull could throw him. When Pecos Bill came to Kansas, he went looking for a challenge. There, he saw a tornado. He jumped on the tornado and held on. The tornado twisted and whirled. It picked up cows, barns, fences, and rivers, but it could not throw Pecos Bill. At last, the tornado gave up. "Neither beast nor storm has a chance against me," boasted Pecos Bill, meaning if a person is determined, he or she can beat just about anything.

Kansas's Sports Teams

Although no professional sports teams play in Kansas, sports fan enjoy plenty of college sports action.

COLLEGE SPORTS

The University of Kansas (KU) in Lawrence has a long and honored sports tradition, especially in basketball. Dr. James Naismith became the university's athletic director

The KU Jayhawks made it to the championship game of the 2003 NCAA Tournament, only to lose to Syracuse University.

Jim Ryun

Jim Ryun from Wichita was one of the fastest runners of all time. In 1965 he set a national high school record for running a mile in 3 minutes and 55.3 seconds, a record that remained until May 2001. In 1966 he set the world's record for running a mile in 3 minutes and 51.3 seconds.

in 1898, not long after he invented the game of basketball in Springfield, Massachusetts. Since then, basketball has been a winning sport for the KU Jayhawks.

The Jayhawks won national titles in 1922, 1923, 1952, and 1988. In 1952 center Clyde Lovellette scored 33 points and Kansas beat St. John's by a score of 80 to 63. That year, Lovellette became the first player in NCAA history to lead the nation in scoring and win an NCAA title in the same season. His accomplishment has yet to be matched.

During the mid-1950s Wilt Chamberlain, a powerful and talented seven-foot center, led the basketball team. After leaving KU, Chamberlain enjoyed a career in the National Basketball Association (NBA), where he was voted most valuable player four times while playing for the Philadelphia 76ers and Los Angeles Lakers.

Lynette Woodard became the first woman at KU to be an all-American for each of her four seasons (1977–1981). Her career total of 3,640 points is a school record. She became the first woman to play for the Harlem Globetrotters.

In 1984 Lynette Woodard captained the U.S. Olympic team that earned a gold medal in women's basketball.

Kansas's Businesses and Products

Kansas is not just fields of wheat and corn. Today, the aerospace industry is Kansas's largest employer, employing about 35,000 people in the Wichita area alone.

FACTORIES

The largest employer in Kansas, Boeing Aircraft Wichita, employs more than 13,000 workers and builds parts for the Boeing 737 and for military jets. Many smaller Wichita companies supply parts and materials to Boeing. The value of all manufactured goods shipped from Kansas each year is more than $40 billion. Other aircraft manufacturers in Kansas include Cessna, Learjet, and Beechcraft. Wichita is also home to the Coleman Company, famous for making camping equipment and coolers.

Raytheon Corp., located in Wichita, is manufacturer of the world's longest continuously running aircraft line—the famed Beech since 1947.

FARM PRODUCTS

Kansas's farms and ranches produce cattle, wheat, corn, and hogs. Farming and ranching contribute about $2.2 billion each year to the state economy. Kansas is the

H&R Block

In the United States, all workers must submit an income tax form to the federal government's Internal Revenue Service (IRS). However, many people find the tax forms confusing, complicated, or time-consuming. In 1955 brothers Henry and Richard Block from Mission Hills began a business that revolutionized tax preparation in this country. They came up with a quick and affordable service that helped people prepare their tax forms for the IRS. Today, H&R Block has thousands of offices across the country.

largest producer of wheat in the world. Sumner County is the wheat capital of the state. Kansas produces about twenty percent of the nation's wheat each year.

Besides leading the world in wheat production, Kansas also leads the world in grain storage. Two of the world's largest grain elevators, where wheat is stored in tall silos, are in Kansas City and in Hutchinson in southwestern Kansas. The Hutchinson grain elevator is more than a half mile in length. It can hold 46 million bushels of grain. Overall, Kansas produces enough wheat to give every person on the planet six loaves of bread each year.

Kansas is one of the top ten oil-producing states.

OIL, GAS, AND MINING

Kansas was the first state west of the Mississippi River to set up oil-drilling operations. It began in 1892. Today, Kansas produces more than 30 million barrels of oil each year.

Kansas produces about 560 billion cubic feet of natural gas each year, valued at more than $2 billion. Natural gas provides fuel for power-generating plants and for home cooking and heating. The Hugoton Gas Field, located in southwestern Kansas, is the largest natural gas field in the United States.

Attractions and Landmarks

Kansas's attractions and landmarks attract visitors who wish to know more about the state's unique past and natural features.

Charles Lindbergh, or "Lindy," was the first man to fly solo across the Atlantic Ocean. When Amelia Earhart became the first woman to fly solo across the Atlantic Ocean, some journalists nicknamed her "Lady Lindy."

*About 60 people still live in Nicodemus. Every July they celebrate the **Emancipation** Proclamation, which freed slaves in most of the United States.*

MUSEUMS AND HISTORIC DISTRICTS

The Amelia Earhart Birthplace Museum is in Atchison, in northeastern Kansas. The house has been restored to look like it did when "America's First Lady of Flying" was born there in 1897. It was originally built in 1861, making it one of the oldest houses in the state. There, one can see furniture, clothes, and other household items that belonged to the Earhart family.

The Nicodemus Historic District is the only remaining town established by African Americans during

Places to See in Kansas

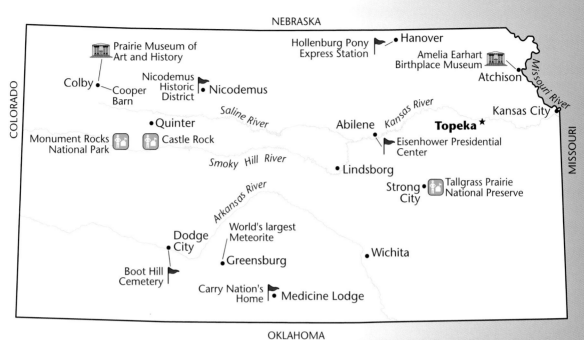

NEBRASKA

Prairie Museum of Art and History

Hollenburg Pony Express Station

Hanover

Amelia Earhart Birthplace Museum

Atchison

COLORADO

Colby

Cooper Barn

Nicodemus Historic District

Nicodemus

Saline River

Kansas River

Kansas City

Abilene

Topeka ★

Eisenhower Presidential Center

Quinter

MISSOURI

Monument Rocks National Park

Castle Rock

Smoky Hill River

Lindsborg

Arkansas River

Strong City

Tallgrass Prairie National Preserve

World's largest Meteorite

Dodge City

Greensburg

Wichita

Boot Hill Cemetery

Carry Nation's Home

Medicine Lodge

OKLAHOMA

★ Capital

• City

River

Historic Sites/Landmark

Museum

National Parks, Forests, and Memorials

N
W   E
S

| 0 | 50 Miles |
| 0 | 50 Kilometers |

Dwight David Eisenhower's Boyhood Home, Abilene

World War II hero and 34th president, Dwight David Eisenhower spent his youth in north-central Kansas. Born in Texas, Eisenhower moved to the cattle town of Abilene when he was eight years old. He lived there from 1898 until 1911, when he left to attend the U.S. Military Academy in West Point, New York. Members of his family lived in Abilene until 1946. "The proudest thing I can claim is that I am from Abilene," said Eisenhower. The family home, along with a library and museum, is now part of the Eisenhower Presidential Center.

41

The Hollenburg Pony Express Station is outside the town of Hanover, in north-central Kansas. Six rooms downstairs contain a store, a kitchen, and bedrooms. There is a large upstairs room where Pony Express riders slept.

the **Reconstruction Era** (1865–1877). Located in northwestern Kansas, it was founded on September 17, 1877. Between 1873 and 1880 eleven similar African American communities thrived in Kansas. The town symbolizes the spirit of the men and women who set out for freedom and new opportunities. In 1976 Congress made Nicodemus a National Historic Site to preserve its history.

Built in 1857, the Hollenburg Pony Express Station is the only original Pony Express station still standing. It was built when riders delivered mail across the country, before railroads took over the

Dodge City

Today, cattle towns such as Abilene and Dodge City celebrate their Wild West history. Dodge City reconstructed its old main street that dates from the 1870s. It has wooden sidewalks, a general store, a blacksmith shop, and horses kept in corrals. Visitors get a sense of what life was like when cowhands brought thousands of cattle through town. Also in Dodge City is Boot Hill Cemetery, first established in about 1873. About six years later, the cemetery was moved to make room for the growing town.

job. At that time, it was the westernmost station in Kansas. Until 1859 it was also the westernmost stop for the railroad and telegraph. After 1859 the railroad and telegraph moved further west, eventually reaching the Pacific coast. The station includes an exhibit that gives information about the brief but exciting Pony Express period.

The Prairie Museum of Art and History is in Colby, in northwestern Kansas. It contains a large collection of historic items found in local homes and on area ranches and farms. Outside the museum stands the Cooper Barn, the largest barn in Kansas. Measuring 66 feet wide, 114 feet long, and 48 feet high, it was moved in one piece to the museum and it houses an exhibit called "From Prairie Grasses to Golden Grain," which traces the history of the area back to the 1870s.

NATURAL WONDERS

The world's largest **meteorite** can be found in Greensburg, in southwestern Kansas. It weighs more than 1,000 pounds. Scientists believe it fell to Earth about 2,000 years ago.

Monument Rocks are about 70 feet tall. They are also known as the Chalk Pyramids, because they are made of sun-baked limestone that is eroded by the wind.

Castle Rock towers 70 feet high, making it a natural landmark that is visible for miles.

The National Park Service designated Monument Rocks Natural Area in northwest Kansas as the first natural landmark in the United States in 1968. These towering chalk structures date back 80 million years, when a sea covered the area. The park is rich in **fossils,** including those belonging to pterosaurs, a large, flying reptile. Thousands of fossilized shark teeth dot the area.

Not far from Monument Rocks is Castle Rock. Near the town of Quinter, Castle Rock was formed from sand and minerals left from an ancient sea about 80 million years ago. It has steep rock walls and flat tops.

Map of Kansas

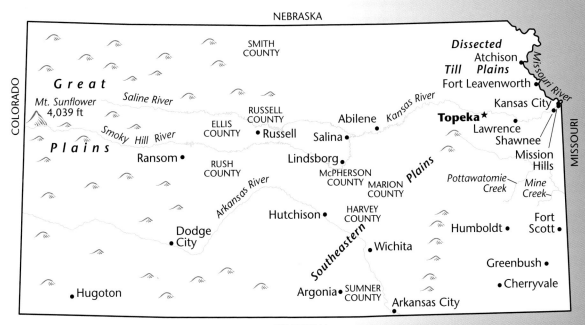

NEBRASKA

SMITH COUNTY

Dissected
Atchison
Till Plains
Fort Leavenworth

Missouri River

Great

Mt. Sunflower
4,039 ft

Saline River

Kansas City

Kansas River

Topeka ★

Lawrence
Shawnee

Smoky Hill River

ELLIS COUNTY

RUSSELL COUNTY

Abilene

Plains

• Russell

Salina •

Mission Hills

Ransom •

RUSH COUNTY

Lindsborg

Pottawatomie Creek

Mine Creek

Arkansas River

McPHERSON COUNTY

MARION COUNTY

Plains

COLORADO

MISSOURI

Hutchison •

HARVEY COUNTY

Humboldt •

Fort Scott •

Dodge
• City

Southeastern

• Wichita

Greenbush •

• Cherryvale

• Hugoton

Argonia •

SUMNER COUNTY

Arkansas City •

OKLAHOMA

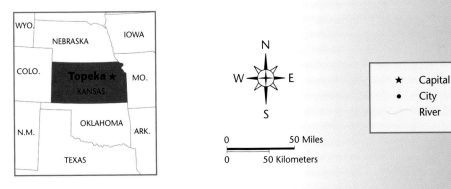

WYO.

NEBRASKA

IOWA

COLO.

Topeka ★
KANSAS

MO.

N.M.

OKLAHOMA

ARK.

TEXAS

N
W — E
S

| 0 | 50 Miles |
| 0 | 50 Kilometers |

★ Capital
• City
～ River

Glossary

appellate court   a court that has the power to hear court appeals and review court decisions

aquifer   a large underground reserve of water

bill   the draft of a law presented for approval to a legislature

bluffs   steep cliffs

Civil War   the war between the Northern states, called the Union, and the Southern states, known as the Confederacy, that was fought between 1861 and 1865

conservationist   a person who works to prevent the loss, or damage of natural resources, such as forests, soil, and water

contiguous   sharing a common boundary

dirigibles   lighter-than-air airships; blimps or zeppelins

discrimination   laws or actions that favor one group of people over another group of people

drought   extended period without rain

Dust Bowl   the name given to much of the Great Plains in the 1930s because a drought dried out the land, resulting in huge dust storms, thereby causing severe erosion of farmland

elevation   height of the land above sea level

emancipation   the act of freeing enslaved people

Emmy Award   an award given to outstanding television performers

erosion   the wearing away of land by wind, water, or ice

extinction   the act of no longer existing

fossils   mineralized remains of ancient plants or animals

Harlem Renaissance   the period from about 1919 to 1935 that saw growth in popular appreciation of African American culture, including poetry and jazz. The period is named after Harlem, a New York City neighborhood that became the center of urban African American life.

Ice Age   a long period marked by extensive cold

jury   a group of people who determine the guilt or innocence of someone accused of committing a crime

legislature   a group of elected officials that makes laws for a state or nation

Louisiana Territory   a large area of land purchased in 1803 by the United States from France. The present-day states of Louisiana, Arkansas, Missouri, Iowa, North Dakota, South Dakota, Nebraska, Kansas, and parts of Minnesota, Oklahoma, Colorado, Wyoming, Montana, and Idaho were carved from the territory.

meteorite   a rocky mass from outer space that reaches Earth

Pulitzer Prize   annual prize given for the best work by journalists and creative writers

Reconstruction Era the period from 1865 to 1877, during which the states of the Confederacy were controlled by the federal government before being readmitted to the Union

reservoir a natural or man-made structure that holds a large amount of water

segregation the practice of separating people of different races in schools, housing, and industry, especially as a way of discriminating against people of color in a mostly white society

slavery a system in which people are permitted to own other people

survey to measure a parcel, or portion, of land to determine its boundaries

tax money raised by the government to pay for services

World War II the largest armed conflict of the 1900s. It began when Germany invaded its European neighbors and Japan invaded its Asian neighbors. The United States entered the war in 1941, after its naval base at Pearl Harbor, Hawaii, was attacked by Japanese warplanes. The war ended in 1945 with the surrenders of Germany and Japan.

More Books to Read

Bale, Karen, and Kathleen Duey. *Trainwreck: Kansas, 1892.* New York: Aladdin, 1999.

Chu, Daniel, and Bill Shaw. *Going Home to Nicodemus: The Story of an African American Frontier Town and the Pioneers Who Settled It.* New York: Messner, 1995.

Gaeddert, Louann. *Friends and Enemies.* New York: Atheneum, 2000.

Jennings, Richard. *The Great Whale of Kansas.* Boston: Houghton Mifflin, 2001.

Seely, Debra. *Grasslands.* New York: Holiday Books, 2002.

Index

About the Author

Larry Bograd is the author of many books for children and young adults. Born in Denver, Colorado, he has traveled extensively throughout Kansas.